EXTREME SURVIVAL
MOUNTAINS

Angela Royston

Chrysalis
Children's Books

EXTREME FACTS

Look for the snow-topped mountain in boxes like this. Here you will find extra facts, stories and information about mountains.

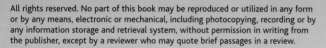

First published in the UK in 2003 by
Chrysalis Children's Books
64 Brewery Road, London N7 9NT

Copyright © Chrysalis Books Plc 2003

Design and editorial production
Bender Richardson White, Uxbridge

A Belitha Book

ISBN 1 84138 699 5

British Library Cataloguing in Publication Data for this book is available from the British Library.

10 9 8 7 6 5 4 3 2 1

Acknowledgements
We wish to thank the following individuals and organizations for their help and assistance and for supplying material in their collections:
CORBIS Corporation/Images: pages 3, 6, 13 top, 15 bottom (Annie Poole; Papillio/CORBIS), 21 right (Galen Rowell/CORBIS), 23 (Galen Rowell/CORBIS), 27 (Bettmann/CORBIS). Ecoscene: pages 10 top (Papilio/Peter Bond), 11 (Matthew Bolton), 29 (Papilio/Peter Bond). Oxford Scientific Films Photo Library: pages 4 (Colin Monteath), 5 (Martyn Colbeck), 6 right (Patrick Morris), 8 (Philippe Poulet), 9 left (Colin Monteath/Hedgehog House), 9 right (Waina Cheng), 12 (Daniel Cox), 13 bottom (Tom Ulrich), 14 Mark Jones, 15 top (Mike Hill), 16 top (Richard Packwood), 16 bottom (Colin Monteath), 19 bottom (Ted Levin/AA), 20 (Doug Allan), 21 left (Philippe Poulet), 22 (Philippe Poulet), 23 left (Francis Lepine/AA), 25 top (Colin Monteath), 25 bottom (Doug Allan), 26 (Konrad Wothe). PhotoDisc Inc.: pages 1 (Jeremy Woodhouse), 2 (Adalberto Rios Szalay/Sexto Sol), 19 top (Adalberto Rios Szalay/Sexto Sol), 28 (Robert Glusic), 30 (Glen Allison), 31 (Glen Allison). Still Pictures: pages 17 (Max Milligan), 18 (Max Milligan), 24 (Hartmut Schwarzbach). Cover photos: Front and back cover: Oxford Scientific Films Photo Library (Colin Monteath)

Diagrams and maps: Stefan Chabluk.

Editorial Manager: Joyce Bentley
Project Editor: Lionel Bender
Text Editor: Clare Hibbert
Design and Make-up: Ben White
Picture Research: Cathy Stastny
Production: Kim Richardson
Consultant: John Stidworthy

We have checked the records in this book but new ones are often added.

Printed in China

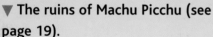

▼ The ruins of Machu Picchu (see page 19).

CONTENTS

▶ The puma, is one
of the largest
mountain predators.

HIGH PLACES

Mountains are places that are much higher than the land around them. The tops of high mountains are some of the hardest places on Earth to survive, for animals and plants, as well as for people.

A mountain is a huge mass of rock that rises into the sky. The lower parts may be covered with trees and plants, but the upper parts are usually bare and covered with snow all year round. Even mountains in hot countries near the Equator have snowy peaks.

▼ This mountaineer is tackling a steep rock face in Mount Cook National Park, New Zealand.

HOW HIGH?

A mountain is usually measured by its altitude, or height, above the surface of the sea. Mount Everest in Nepal, central Asia, is the world's highest mountain. Its peak, or summit, is 8848m above sea level.

Most of the world's highest mountains are part of a group, or range, of mountains. The highest range is the Himalayas, and the longest is the Andes. The Rocky Mountains, or Rockies, are the highest mountains in North America.

Some plants, animals and people are adapted to living on a mountain. Others have found ways of surviving the extreme conditions there. Some people also visit mountains for fun. They enjoy the challenges of climbing – and standing 'on top of the world'.

▲ Mount Everest is majestic and awe-inspiring. But it is also one of the most dangerous places on Earth. Strong winds deter most climbers.

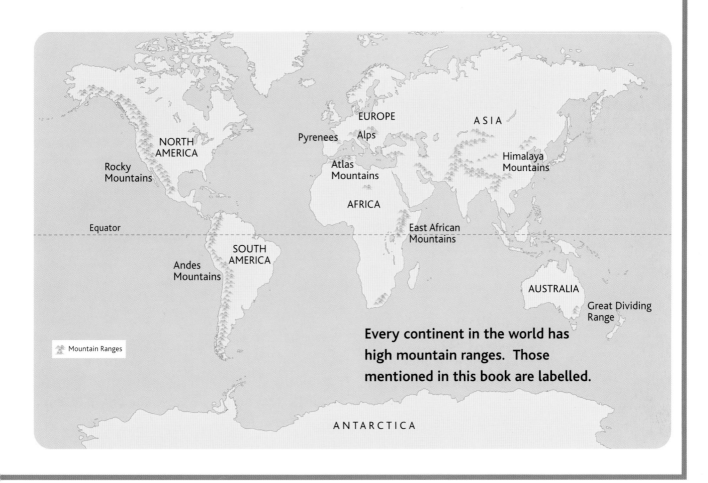

Every continent in the world has high mountain ranges. Those mentioned in this book are labelled.

GOING UP

Mountainsides become colder the higher you climb. The plants you see change too. The air also becomes thinner, so there is less oxygen for living things to breathe.

As you go north or south from the Equator, the countryside changes – from desert to grasslands, temperate forest, tundra and finally to icy poles.

As you climb a high mountain, climate and habitats change in a similar way. Plants on the lowest slopes are the same as those in the surrounding area. But as the temperature drops, broad-leaved trees, such as maples, are replaced by conifers, such as pine trees. Above a height known as the tree line, not even conifers grow. The animals that live in each habitat change, too.

◀ Wapiti – a relative of the Red deer – can survive the bleak conditions on Arctic mountains in North America and Asia.

▲ Giant senecios grow above the tree line on Mount Kenya. They do not shed dead leaves – these protect the trunks from freezing.

Above the tree line, only grass and low, scrubby plants grow. There are fewer animals, too. Higher still is the snow line. Above this, the bare rocks of the mountain are covered with ice and snow all year round, just as in the Arctic.

ABOVE THE CLOUDS
The highest peaks soar above the clouds. Only commercial airliners fly above the top of Mount Everest.

Snow line about 4500m

Golden eagle

Habitats of the Rocky Mountains

◀ **Like all high mountains, the Rockies have different habitats – living areas – going up the slopes. Each level has a different community of plants and animals.**

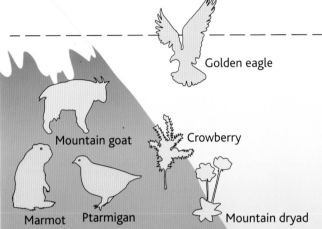

Mountain goat

Crowberry

Marmot   Ptarmigan

Mountain dryad

Treeline, the limit of coniferous trees about 2500m

Spruce

Wolf

Black bear   Elk

Pine

Limit of broad-leaved trees about 800m

Red fox

Squirrel

Deer

Grouse   Hare   Fir   Larch   Aspen

THE MOUNTAIN YEAR

The weather on mountains near the Equator does not change much during the year, but mountains further north and south may go through long, harsh winters and short, chilly summers.

The snow line is the height of the lowest permanent snow. In winter, temperatures on the upper slopes can plummet to –40 °C. Some animals hibernate in underground burrows, while others move further down the mountain for shelter. But even the lower slopes may be covered with snow and experience fierce winds.

▼ Mountains are dangerous places all year round. Maps and compasses help climbers to keep to their route.

▼ With the onset of spring, flowers seem to appear by magic. Aster daisies cover the ground below Chomolonzo in Tibet, central Asia.

▶ A snowstorm, or blizzard, approaches in the Swiss Alps. During a blizzard, the temperature falls and it becomes impossible to see very far.

SCARY FOOTSTEPS

Giant footprints have been spotted in the snow in the Himalayas. Some people say they come from a creature called the abominable snowman or yeti – but they are probably made by a bear or another large animal.

When spring comes, the snow begins to melt in the sunshine. Flowers bloom on the grassy slopes and animals move back up the mountain from the forests. In summer, farmers bring their cows, sheep and goats to the higher slopes to graze.

Mountaineers plan their climbs to make use of the summer weather. This is when conditions are best for climbing, but weather on the high slopes can still be wintry. Climbers may be stuck in blizzards for days at a time and avalanches are frequent.

TOUGH PLANTS

Plants that grow on the steep mountain slopes above the tree line have to be tough to survive. In addition, they have only a short summer in which to flower and produce seeds.

The cold temperatures mean that mountain, or alpine, plants grow very slowly. Plants on the high slopes are low-growing to keep out of the wind. They have long roots to reach down and bind to soil beneath the rocks. They also have small leaves and strong, woody stems. Some plants find shelter from the wind by growing in cracks in the rocks.

▶ Alpine flowers, like this Creeping avens in Austria, are brightly coloured to attract the few insects around for pollination.

▼ Cabbage groundsels and a giant lobelia on Mount Kenya. Their leaves are good at trapping the little rainwater that falls.

The leaves, stems and even the flowers of many high mountain plants are covered with fine hairs. The hairs trap warmth, protecting the plant from the cold, but still let through light so the leaves can make food. Some mountain plants have thick leaves that store water before it drains down the mountainside. When warm weather comes, mountain plants quickly form flowers and seeds before the deathly cold returns.

▶ Mountain plants above the tree line form mounds to survive the wind. This plant is a yareta, growing high in the Bolivian Andes.

RAIN SHADOW

Most rain is carried by clouds that blow from the ocean. Clouds often drop all their rain on the ocean side of the mountain. This means that the other side of the mountain can be extremely dry. Plants here need to cope with little water.

ANIMAL SURVIVORS

Animals that live on the high mountain slopes have to survive extreme cold and steep, uneven ground. Plants are small and spread out over a wide area, so animals work hard to find enough food.

▼ Timber wolves hunt in packs. A wolf can hear and smell its prey up to 10 km away.

Some small, furry creatures feed on the grasses that grow on the high mountainsides. Among them, marmots hibernate in winter, storing food as body fat well in advance of the cold weather. Chinchillas are active through the year.

Wild sheep and goats find footholds on even the steepest slopes. Large-horned Dall's sheep roam the Alaskan Range. Vicunas graze high in the Andes. They are related to camels, and have thick, fine wool that keeps them warm.

HUNTED DOWN
Mountain animals have been hunted to virtual extinction for their warm, fur coats. From chinchillas to Snow leopards, many mountain creatures are now rare in their natural habitats.

Meat-eaters prowl the slopes on the lookout for prey. Food is so scarce that only a few predators can survive on any mountain. Snow leopards live in the Himalayas while pumas are still found in parts of the Rockies. On the Alaskan Range, timber wolves hunt Dall's sheep. Often they scavenge, feeding on animals that are dead or dying.

▼ The lynx hunts birds, rabbits and rodents in the mountains of North America. It makes dens under rocks or in caves.

▼ Bighorn sheep are at home on mountain slopes in North America. Their small feet can fit between rocks, making them sure-footed.

HIGH FLIERS

Mountain birds have to combat strong, cold winds. The highest flyers – condors and eagles – make use of the wind's currents to soar across the peaks.

These huge, powerful birds keep a keen eye out for food. They soar high in the sky then, on seeing prey, swoop down. Condors are a kind of vulture and feed on dead animals. Eagles feed on such live prey as rabbits and sheep, which they kill with their sharp, curved talons and beak.

GIANT, FLESH-EATING BIRDS

From tip to tip, the Californian condor's wings are 2.9m across, making it North America's largest bird. The Andean condor is even larger – its outstretched wings measure 3m across.

▶ A condor glides among the mountaintops of the Andes. This beautiful bird has a taste for dead flesh.

Small birds, such as the Mountain plover, are thrown about by the wind. Most keep close to the ground. Some hide in burrows at night to escape the coldest temperatures. Others, such as the Diuca finches in the Andes, huddle under rocks to keep warm.

Butterflies arrive in summer to feed on alpine flowers. Many are blown up the mountain, providing welcome food for other insects and spiders. Only a few insects thrive in the cold. Rock crawlers look a bit like cockroaches. Nicknamed ice bugs, they die if the weather becomes too warm!

▶ White-tailed ptarmigans live on the Rocky Mountains. Their feet are feathered to help them walk across the snow.

▼ An Alpine chough, a type of crow, perches on a rocky outcrop in the Swiss Alps. The chough feeds on worms and insects.

MOUNTAIN PEOPLE

Mountain people are strong survivors. Their bodies and way of life have adapted so they can meet the challenge of life high above the rest of the world.

One difficulty that mountain people face is the thin air. Each breath they take contains less of the oxygen that all living things need to survive. So their bodies have adapted. Their lungs are bigger, so they have a larger capacity for taking in oxygen. And their hearts are bigger, so they can pump extra oxygen-carrying blood.

▲ People often build terraces, or giant steps, into the side of the mountain. The flat terraces are easier to farm. These terraces are on Madeira Island.

◄ People use yaks to carry goods through the Himalayas. The animals are adapted to life at high altitudes – they have a thick coat that allows them to survive at −40°C.

16

Many mountain people follow a traditional way of life. Sherpas live in north-western Nepal. They keep yaks that provide milk, food and skin to make warm clothes. Sherpas also plant rice, barley and other crops. Instead of tractors, they use yaks to pull their ploughs.

TENZING AT THE TOP

One of the first people to scale Mount Everest was a sherpa – a Nepalese mountain guide. Tenzing Norgay reached the summit with the New Zealander, Edmund Hillary, on the 29 May 1953.

▲ Many mountains are holy places. These pilgrims are climbing Qolquepinktes in Peru to collect sacred ice for a religious festival.

More and more mountain people make a living from tourists and climbers. Some sell clothes or blankets. Others act as guides to trekkers. Sherpas act as porters, too, carrying heavy equipment across the Himalayas.

MAKING A LIVING

When they are not acting as guides, mountain people live by farming the land or mining. People have lived high in the mountains for thousands of years.

Most mountain people are farmers who live on plateaus or in valleys. In summer they take their sheep, goats and cattle higher up the mountain to graze. Animals provide milk, which can be made into cheese, and meat. High in the Andes, around Lake Titicaca, people fish, too. The lake is the highest in the world.

▶ This Andean mother and child are harvesting potatoes. Both are warmly dressed and the mother wears a traditional hat.

 POTATO DIET
The first people to eat potatoes lived in the Andes. About 12 000 years ago, South American Indians began to cultivate the potatoes that grew wild there.

Many mountains are rich in minerals. In Peru and Bolivia, people mine copper, lead, silver, zinc and tin. People in mining towns live in stone houses with thick walls to keep out the cold. They wear warm clothes of wool or animal skin. Most paths are too steep and rough for vehicles, so people may use animals to carry their loads. There are also railways to carry people to the mines.

▼ In the Andes, a llama provides its owner with transport, milk and wool for clothes.

▲ Machu Picchu is a large, ruined mountain city in Peru. It was built by the Incas – South American Indians who had an empire in Peru that was destroyed by Spanish conquerors in the early 1500s.

PLANNING A CLIMB

Every year, experienced mountaineers scale the world's highest peaks, from Alaska to the Himalayas. They must be extremely fit, healthy and well-prepared.

▼ This is the base camp on Mount Everest. The final plans for the attempt on the summit are made here.

It takes months to plan an expedition. The leaders work out the route. They raise money to pay for guides, equipment and supplies. They also choose the members of the expedition. Each will be an experienced climber who can cope with high altitudes.

Mountaineers have to survive extreme cold and severe storms. They are trained to look out for frostbite. This happens when parts of the body – especially toes, fingers, ears and noses – freeze solid.

Altitude sickness is another hazard. Climbers spend a few weeks climbing at about 6000m to allow their bodies to adapt to the lack of oxygen. At first their heart beats fast and they are soon out of breath. After a few days, their blood begins to produce more red blood cells to take in more oxygen.

MOUNTAIN SICKNESS

At 5200m the air contains half the amount of oxygen than it does at sea level. Lack of oxygen causes altitude sickness. It affects the body and brain and, if it continues for days, can be fatal.

▼ **Avalanches, as here in the Himalayas, are a hazard for mountain climbers. Warmth or disturbance can cause tonnes of snow to loosen and tumble downhill at great speed and without warning.**

▶ **This climber is well-equipped for a few days on the mountains. Careful planning is essential.**

Helmet – to protect the head from falling rocks.

Backpack – tent, sleeping bag, cooking equipment and food must be carried.

Snow suit – lightweight but wind and snow proof jacket and trousers.

Ropes, clamps and ice-axe – to help clamber up steep slopes and ice fields.

Boots – with spikes on the soles to dig into compact snow and ice.

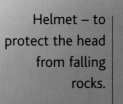

CLIMBING KIT

A mountaineering expedition needs an extraordinary amount of equipment. There are tents and camping gear, climbing equipment and supplies.

The route to the top almost always involves cliff faces, overhangs and glaciers. Climbers wear crampons – metal spikes that fit to climbing boots to give extra grip on ice. They carry ropes, so they can rope themselves together. Then, if one climber slips, they cannot fall too far.

Climbers also carry several litres of drinking water – they would die if they went too long without fresh water. Depending on the duration of their climb, they also take supplies of food.

◀ Climbing sheer, or vertical, rock faces takes courage. This mountaineer is free-climbing, setting a rope for her partner down below.

CHEATING?

Bottles of oxygen were first used by climbers in the Himalayas in the 1920s. Some climbers thought that using oxygen was cheating. Today, a few climbers are again trying to climb without it.

◀ This climber uses an ice axe to cut footholds, and crampons on his boots to grip the rock.

Climbers also need warm clothes. These are made of lightweight materials that keep body heat in and cold air, wind and moisture out.

Most climbers use oxygen tanks on the highest slopes. The tanks are heavy to carry, but the extra oxygen allows them to climb more quickly and in thinner air. A tank contains only enough oxygen for a limited time, so climbers have to make sure that they do not run out.

▲ An expedition doctor checks oxygen bottles used to provide extra oxygen in the thin mountain air.

MOUNTAIN CAMPS

Most members of a climbing expedition never try to reach the summit. Their job is to carry supplies up the mountainside and establish camps along the route.

High mountains are too tall to climb in a day. The climb can take days, weeks or even longer in bad weather. The expedition usually sets up a base camp at around 5200m, then more camps further up the mountain. Eventually two or three mountaineers climb from the last camp to make the attempt on the summit.

▲ In the Himalayas in central Asia, local people known as sherpas often act as porters and guides. They carry backpacks up to the mountain camps.

Climbers use portable stoves to make hot food and drinks. They wear layers of clothes to protect themselves against hypothermia – a condition that occurs as one's body temperature falls. At first the person becomes confused and may even take off some clothes. When a person's body temperature falls below 32°C, he or she becomes unconscious. If it falls below 25°C, the person may die. Climbers are most at risk of hypothermia if they have an accident or are caught in an avalanche.

MOUNTAIN LITTER

Reaching the summit is not the end of the expedition. The mountaineers still have to climb back down safely. But often they do not have the time or strength to bring all their equipment down from each camp. The rest is left and becomes litter.

▲ Many mountaintops, like this one in Nepal, are being damaged and polluted by the people who visit them.

▼ These climbers in the Himalayas have stopped to eat. They have put up a small tent in case they need shelter.

MOUNTAINS: FACTS

WHICH IS THE HIGHEST?

Mount Everest is the highest mountain above sea level at 8848m. Mauna Kea in Hawaii rises 10 203m from its base on the sea bed but only 4205m of this are above sea level.

CONTINENTAL GIANTS

Mount McKinley (6194m) in Alaska is the highest mountain in North America. Aconcagua (6959m) in the Andes is South America's highest.

Russia's Mount Elbrus (5642m) is the highest in Europe. Kilimanjaro (5895m), in Tanzania, is Africa's highest mountain. Australasia's highest is Mount Wilhelm (4509m).

DROPPING TEMPERATURE

The temperature on a mountainside falls about 0.5°C for every 100m in height. The cooling effect of winds, known as the wind factor, makes the upper mountain slopes colder still.

▶ Climbing a glacier in the mountains of Argentina.

▶ Sherpa Tenzing Norgay (left) and Edmund Hillary with their medals and awards for being the first people to reach the top of Mount Everest in 1953.

ALPINE SNOW-MELTER

The alpine snowbell, which is native to Europe, grows under the snow. In spring its dark flower buds absorb enough sunlight to melt the layer of snow above them. Some other alpine plants can do this, too.

COLOUR CHANGE

Some mountain animals, such as the Mountain hare, stay on the high slopes all year round. The hare's fur is white in the winter, camouflaging it against the snow from birds of prey. In summer, when the snow melts, its coat changes to brown.

CLIFF-CLIMBING BIRDS

Wall creepers are birds that clamber all over sheer cliffs in search of insects, using their tail for balance. They climb up and down head-first, pushing their thin, curved beak into narrow cracks in search of insects.

FIRST MOUNTAINEERS

Mont Blanc, the highest peak in the Alps at 4807m, was first climbed by two Frenchmen, Michel-Gabriel Paccard and Jacques Balmat in 1786. Mountaineering really took off as a sport during the 1800s.

SNOW CAVE

If climbers are caught in a storm, they need to make a shelter – fast. The quickest way to make a snow cave is to put their bags and equipment in a heap and pile snow over it. They press the snow down hard, then tunnel under it to pull out their bags. The space left is their cave.

MOUNTAINS: SUMMARY

Mountains present living things with extreme conditions ranging from lack of oxygen and strong winds to temperatures far below freezing.

Some mountain animals and plants have a natural covering that traps warmth and keeps out the cold. Other animals live on the mountain slopes only in summer, then move to lower, warmer levels for the winter. Some small mammals hibernate or live in burrows during winter. People survive on mountains only if they can cope with the lack of oxygen and have sufficiently warm clothing. Disturbance or pollution of mountains by foresters, climbers and hikers upsets this extreme environment.

▼ High in the mountains of Greenland, meltwater from glaciers, ice fields and snow that covers the summits forms crystal-clear lakes of fresh water.

MOUNTAINS: ON THE WEB

You can visit mountains on the Internet. Here are listed some good sites where you can find out more about extreme conditions on mountains, mountain wildlife and mountaineering. Websites can change, so if you cannot find all those listed, look for other sites on the subject via a search engine by typing in keywords such as 'mountains' or 'alpine'.

Mount Everest
www.mnteverest.net/
Information on Mount Everest in the Himalayas and on climbing expeditions to the region.

Denali National Park
www.nps.gov/dena/
More information on the Alaskan Range and its wildlife.

Aconcagua
www.aconcagua.com/
This site focuses on Aconcagua, the tallest mountain in South America.

International Snow Leopard Trust
www.snowleopard.org
A website about saving the Snow leopard in the mountains of Asia. There is also a short video of this beautiful, big cat.

Amazing animals: Californian condor
www.bbc.co.uk/nature/reallywild/amazing/
    californian_condor.shtml
All about the Californian condor.

Meet the Sherpas
www.teacher.scholastic.com/hillary/archive/
    sherpas.htm
Information about the Sherpas in Nepal, with links to sites about Everest.

Alpine gardening
www.backyardgardener.com/index2.html
This website is about mountain plants and gives advice on how to grow them in your garden.

▼ Creeping avens bursts into flower in spring.

MOUNTAINS: WORDS

This glossary explains some of the words used in this book that you might not have seen before.

Adapted

naturally built to survive.

Alpine

in, on or from the Alps.

Altitude

height above sea level.

Altitude sickness

when a person becomes ill from lack of oxygen, high in the mountains.

Avalanche

a large mass of snow that suddenly slides down the mountainside.

Blizzard

a severe snowstorm with very strong wind.

Climate

the average weather of a place over the year.

Desert

a dry region with very few plants; it may be hot or cold.

Equator

an imaginary line that circles the Earth. This is the hottest region of the Earth, and the part farthest from the poles.

Frostbite

when body parts freeze. Unless frostbite is treated quickly, the flesh dies and has to be cut away.

▶ Wind, ice and melting snow have eroded, or worn away, the top of this mountain into sharp, jagged peaks.

Glacier
a slow-moving river of ice.

Habitat
the place where an animal or plant lives, for example a mountain.

Hibernate
to spend the winter in a sleep-like state, then become active again when conditions improve.

Hypothermia
when a person's body temperature drops too low to function properly.

Mountain range
a chain of mountains that lie alongside each other.

Mountaineering
the sport of climbing mountains.

Overhang
part of a cliff face where rock juts out overhead.

Oxygen
a gas, found in air, which all living things need to breathe to survive.

Plateau
a high, flat area of land.

Predator
an animal that hunts and kills other animals, its prey.

Red blood cells
the parts of the blood that carry oxygen round the body.

Scavenge
to feed on dead or dying animals.

Snow line
the level beyond which the ground is always snow-covered.

Temperate forest
tree-covered region with a mild climate.

Tree line
the level above which it is too cold for trees to grow.

Tundra
treeless area near the Arctic where the ground is frozen all year round.

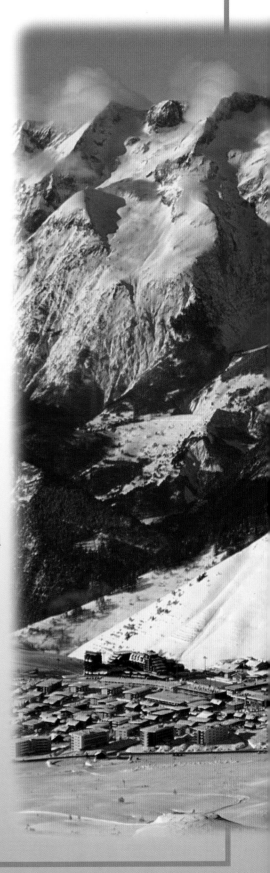

▶ **In mountain areas, villages are often built on plateaus.**

INDEX